★ REGISTERED POETS & ILLUSTRATOR ★
★ STATE OF IMAGINATION ★

DOTLICH,
HEARD &
FREEDMAN

WORD*S*ONG

AN IMPRINT OF ASTRA BOOKS
FOR YOUNG READERS
NEW YORK

2023

WELCOME TO THE
WONDER HOUSE

Poems by **Rebecca Kai Dotlich & Georgia Heard**
Illustrations by **Deborah Freedman**

WORDꟅONG

AN IMPRINT OF ASTRA BOOKS FOR YOUNG READERS
New York

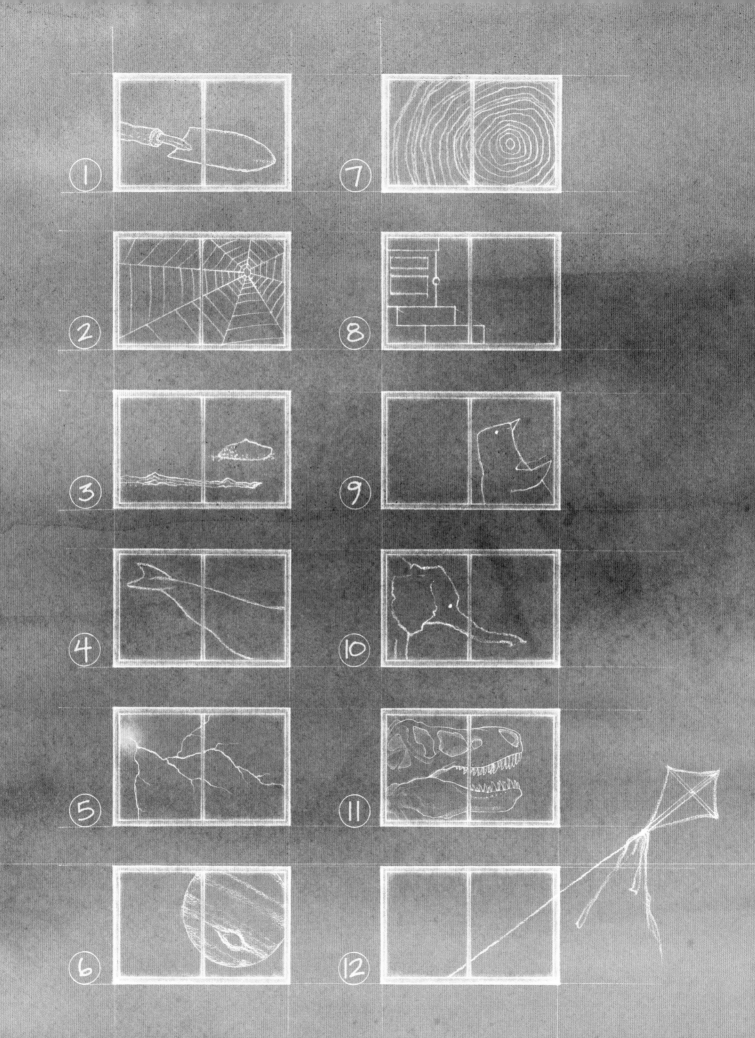

SCALE: 1" = INFINITY

CONTENTS

ROOM OF CURIOSITY

Why do diamonds wink
and shine?
What is quartz?
What is lime?
What fossils still
sleep underground?
How *does* our Earth
keep spinning around?
How bubbling hot
does it get on the sun?
Our oceans: are they all
just one?
What happens when
meteorites collide?
And what have scientists
found inside?
Could Saturn have thousands
of icy rings?
We wonder about so many things!

—RKD

Keep an open heart,
that's where curiosity likes to start.
—GH

ROOM OF PRAISE

Rain is everything
to a worm,
a puddle,
an umbrella.
Small drips
of Sunday's cloud
slip like clear stars spattering
bluewhite skies
onto sidewalks,
skyscrapers,
fields of sugarcane;
oh! Sideswept rain
pinging crystal notes.
Listen.
They are tapping,
        tapping,
unpacking sky . . .

—RKD

In honor of spiders
hiding in dim corners, under rafters
quiet as air, patient as monks,

weaving silk traps—
fine as snowflakes,
strong as steel.

—GH

Sometimes I praise paper,
the way it waits
like crinkled squares of white sky,
open with all that space,

or the way it carries words
from room to room,
wrinkling out a language
of ancient trees,

or the way it is so papery
as it waits for me
to trace my hand
or spill my heart.
Sometimes I praise paper.

—RKD

This stone
has a secret and mysterious life.

Was it cast from a volcano
in some distant past?
What river did it rest by
while sun warmed and rain fell?
What stars bobbed above it?
What curious fish nibbled
next to it, and did it hear
the clanging
of tin pans from a faraway
campground?

What young girl
stuffed it in her pocket,
claimed it as her good luck charm?

—RKD

ORDINARY THINGS

A gnarled stick
clutched in my hand can be:

a thin shovel
to dig for wriggling worms,

a charmed wand
to cast magic spells,

a ruler
to measure how deep a mud puddle dips,

a fishing pole
to catch a fish like the world has never seen,

a pencil
to write the letters of my name in the sand.

—GH

ROOM OF CREATURES

Bodies loose and limp—

    clam

    octopus

    slug

    shrimp

No wonder you squish and squirm—

    snail

    mussel

    jellyfish

    worm

Creatures with no inner skeleton,

wriggle and bob and twist like gelatin.

—GH

Through glass-green skin, a
hiccup of frog's tiny heart
beats valentine red.

—RKD

How do dolphins sleep?
They snooze in salty water—
one eye wide open.

—GH

Bristling centipede,
blue-bubbled man-o'-war,
spitting spittlebug.

Hail to the
hair-raising,
hideous,
weird,
and wild.

—GH

ROOM OF NATURE

Thunder drums the skin of sky,

striking

      an

           electric

                   scar

from cloud to cloud.

—GH

Beneath a trillion leaves
cloud-braided with sky,

my feet balance on a tangle
of puzzled roots in a wilderness of secrets,
of mushrooms and moss and winds;

marveling at twigs curling into one another,
I listen as raindrops speak small lullabies
to birds, beckoning

this whole wide world . . .

—RKD

An entomologist dips a net into a pea-green pond,
studies whirligig beetles twirling
like tiny bumper cars that never touch.

Steering a telescope toward starry skies, an astronomer
spies Jupiter's stormy red eye
among wild squalls of banded clouds.

A geologist measures seismic waves,
considers Earth's core—
a boiling furnace of sizzling rock.

In a lab, a physicist creates soap bubbles,
wobbling gifts of air wrapped in slippery skin
that *POP* in an instant.

An ornithologist scouts sky with binoculars,
spots a bald eagle soaring,
wings spread wider than your open arms.

A glass beaker fizzes, as a chemist
mixes vinegar and baking soda.
Watch out: erupting volcano!

The tiniest, the biggest
mysteries near and beyond,
above and below and inside out,
science is the world we wonder about.

—GH

Crack this crystal rock,
trace these scribbles of old gold:
buried ancient charms.

—RKD

ROOM OF TIME

From tiny trunk to grandfather tree rings circle and circle and circle the center of this pine—a slow clock in a deep forest. —RKD

Turn back Earth's clock,
look at fossils printed in rock.

At least ten thousand years old—
with one croc's skull, a story is told.

In this prehistoric time booth,
see a cracked iguanodon tooth.

Turn back Earth's clock,
fossils are our planet's ticktock.

—GH

Way up in this tree house
with slanted windows,
trapdoors,
a rope ladder to tug
and tuck and hide
so no one else can climb inside,

we can scheme
among limbs and leaves,
spill secrets,
dream forever and tomorrow and tomorrow
beneath a rainstorm
of summer stars.

—RKD

Puzzle-shaped continents and islands
circled by swirls of blue ocean,
turn on this globe I cradle in my hand.
But what I cannot see:
a girl flying a kite,
warm rain falling,
a drop of water in the sea,
a child like me on the other side
of the world, walking to school
spinning a red umbrella.

—GH

PLACE

Hundreds of windows light up this city block:
a family rolls spaghetti on their forks;
a boy plays saxophone, notes
floating down into an alleyway;
a cat sits on a step
batting at snowflakes
flurrying to the street.
I stop to stare.
I wonder if someone
is watching me wondering?

—GH

ROOM OF QUIET

If you travel into space,
lean in to listen:
no whir, no thrum,
no whooshing air,
few molecules to hum and ping—
there is a great stillness between stars.

—GH

Our small boots
like quiet cookie cutters
carve snow prints
on a sidewalk vanished
under lumps of winter.

This small spot,
padded in white and wind,
begs us to listen.

Hush.
We can almost hear the glaze of sky.

—RKD

ROOM OF IMAGINATION

I am drawing a house
deep in a forest I've never seen;

somewhere in a corner,
a hush and a hum have conversation
in the pocket of a warm sweater
that wraps itself
around puppies sleeping near a window.

The chimney nods to the roof
while an elephant in all his grayness
sips from a river
in a picture framed on an invisible wall.

Words tangle themselves into a blessing
on a blue birdhouse hanging
from a make-believe branch
as my pencil carves a moon on the door.

—RKD

This jumble of tumbled dreams;
of blocks and bricks
remembers when they were:
a regal castle with flanking towers
and a yellow drawbridge crossing a moat,
the Great Wall of China
winding like a red dragon's tail
around the room,
a blue rocket—
10 . . .
   9 . . .
      8—
ready to thunder
into space.

—GH

ROOM OF MYSTERY

What was it like
that final day
when all you knew
fell away,

and dinosaur roars,
one by one
went silent, and
then did the sun
explode upon the Earth
that day, a searing sort
of cinder-spray;
and did the world
turn ember blue
as flakes of ash
blew down on you
as meteors
from outer space
sprayed hot pebbles
in your face
and cauterized your tails gray;
what was it *like*
that final day?

—RKD

HELLO? *HELLO??* *HELLO?*

Two trillion galaxies glow in the universe—

Where is everyone?

Are there sprouts of life sailing
in the dusty spiral of the Milky Way?

Are sleeping creatures buried in the icy
lake of a planet's moon?

Are aliens light-years away, sending
signals that haven't reached us yet?

Where is everyone?
Can you hear us?

—GH

MILKY WAY
100-000-LY

ROOM OF WISHES

I wrote my wish
upon a kite,
closed my eyes,
grabbed its string—

through wind
I ran,
let it fly . . .
My wish came true,
it flew into
that wide, wide map
of sky,

and sailed my name
up high and free,
and with it sailed
a part of me.

—RKD

This wish has pedals
to help me fly down a hill;
a pinwheel blur of silver spokes,
a streak of glossy red
taking me
where the breeze whispers
and the sun bubbles
over a small creek,
where splashes amaze tadpoles.
And I can just be
      and be
         and be . . .

—RKD

Where do wishes go,
do they linger in the sky?
Old wishes.
Birthday wishes.
Shooting star wishes.
Wishbone wishes.
Dandelion wishes.
Wise wishes.
World wishes.
Even superhero wishes.

Clouds are crowded with wishes.

—GH

27

The Wonder House

is our whole world.....

A Note About WONDER

We are all born with a sense of wonder. The greatest explorers, scientists, artists, and writers are always on a quest to discover new and remarkable things. The more curious we are, the more questions we have. As we wonder, the world opens up even *more* mysteries for us to marvel at.

You are a wonderer, too, brimming with imagination and creativity. So, grab a notebook, gaze out a window, follow a meandering creek, sit on a step, and look and listen to the ordinary and the extraordinary all around you. You'll find wonder everywhere.

—RKD & GH

Begin a poem

Tell a story

Paint a picture

Imagine you are someone or something else

Peer into a microscope

Build a model

Draw a blueprint

Take a wonder walk

Share your discoveries with a friend

To the memory of my brother Curt, who instilled in me a world of curiosity about countries, cultures, coins, and keys, old houses and marbles and maps. How I wish we would've had more years in the room of time. —*RKD*

To Leo—who opened my heart to a world of wonder ♥ —*GH*

Dedicated, especially the Room of Imagination, to Jane and Richard —*DF*

For information about permission to reproduce selections from this book, please contact permissions@astrapublishinghouse.com.

Wordsong
An imprint of Astra Books for Young Readers,
a division of Astra Publishing House
astrapublishinghouse.com
Printed in China

ISBN: 978-1-63592-762-7 (hc)
ISBN: 978-1-63592-863-1 (eBook)
Library of Congress Control Number: 2022921791

First edition

10 9 8 7 6 5 4 3 2 1

Design by Barbara Grzeslo
The book title and other hand lettering was done by Deborah Freedman.
The text is set in Frutiger LT Std 57.
Room titles are set in Bookman Old Style.
The illustrations are done in mixed media.

What was the first word ever spoken?

How do bubbles get inside of marbles?

Are there undiscovered treasure chests on the ocean floor?

Can an owl really twist its head all the way around?

Is a mood ring magic?

Is there someone on the other side of the world just like me?

What happens when you break the sound barrier?

Where were the first swords made?   How tiny are toadlets?

Who invented the first alphabet?

What are the planets we haven't discovered yet?

Why does time pass so fast when I am sleeping?